Claudine Z. Muller

Guess the hidden English idioms

GUESS THE HIDDEN ENGLISH IDIOMS

GUESS THE HIDDEN ENGLISH IDIOMS

ISBN : 978-2-9575854-1-0

Dépôt légal : Mars 2022

DEDICACE

A mon chéri, pour son amour et son soutien.

SOMETHING

ICE

ON

ICE

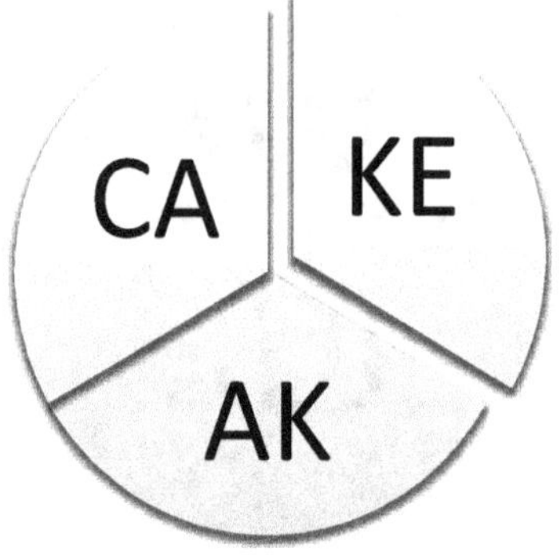
CA
KE
AK

YARDS YARDS YARDS

YARDS YARDS YARDS

YARDS YARDS YARDS

ROOM
ELEPHANT

HUMERUS   TIBIA

ULNA      FIBULA

RADIUS   FEMUR

=

DEDETAVILILS

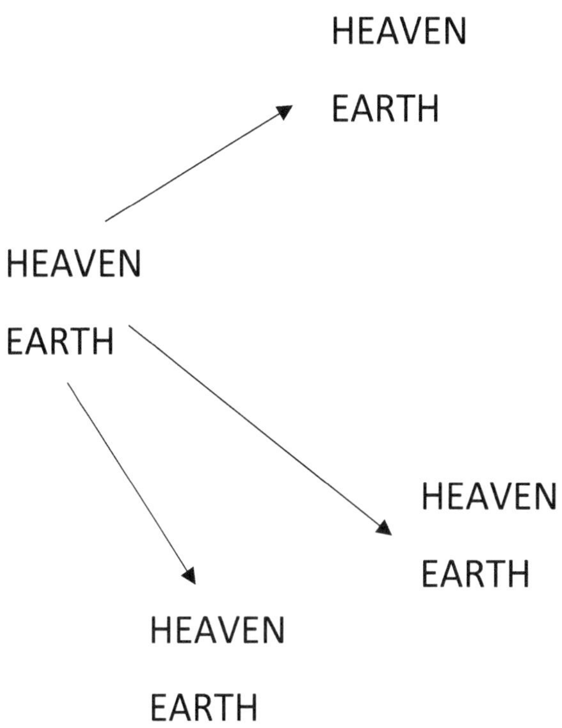

HEAVEN
EARTH
HEAVEN
EARTH
HEAVEN
EARTH
HEAVEN
EARTH

BEANS BEANS

BEANS BEANS

BEANS BEANS

BEANS

BEAN   BEANS

BEANS

BEANS   BEANS

LOOK

YESTERDAY

LEAP

NOW

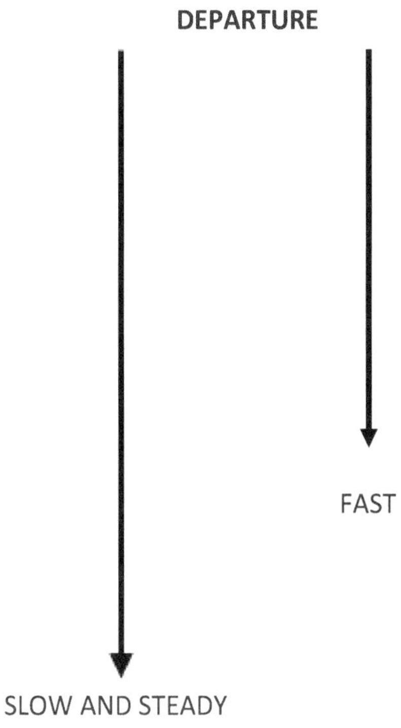

DEPARTURE
FAST
SLOW AND STEADY
ARRIVAL

GOLD

CHIMPANZEE

SUN/RAIN

STAND
STAND
STAND
STAND

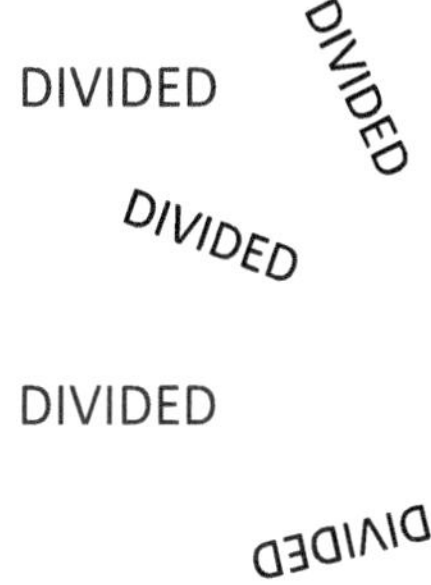

TURTLE

YELLOW

RED

GREEN

BE

PINK

ORANGE

CAUTION

WIND

POCNOC

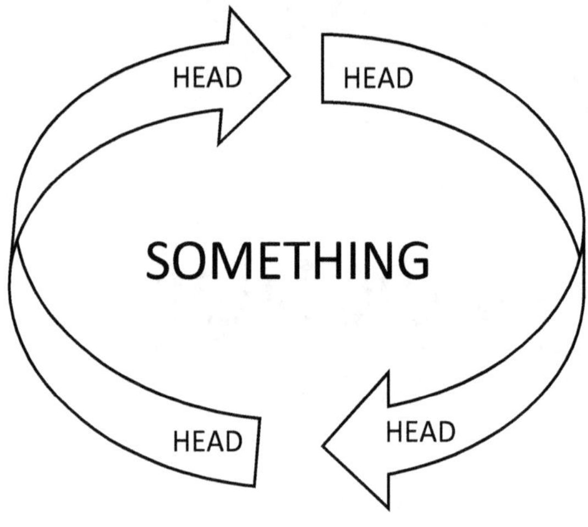

HEAD
HEAD
SOMETHING
HEAD
HEAD

EBUGAR

COW

GRASS GRASS SNAKE GRASS GRASS
GRASS GRASS GRASS GRASS GRASS GRASS

STO

BUTTERFLIESBUTTERFLIESBUTTERFLIES

MACH

MBLOONCEOUEN

BIRD (BLAH ! BLAH ! BLAH !)

_ _ G _ _

B _ _ V _ _

WOOD

WOOD   WOOD

WOOD   WOOD

WOOD

YOU ARE
HERE !

HGEATND

HAND   GET

GO

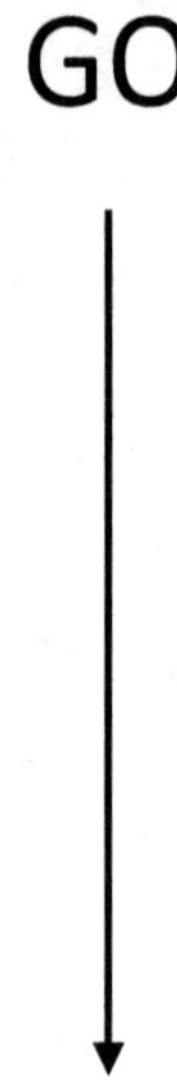

FLAMES FLAMES FLAMES FLAMES FLAMES

Late

Never

SOME   /   BODY

SLACK SLACK SLACK

SLACK SLACK SLACK SLACK

SLACK SLACK SLACK SLACK SLACK

CORNERS

THIEVES

40

BULLET

BDILESSSGINUIGSE

M   N

AD

ESS

M
MA
MAD
MADN
MADNE
MADNES
MADNESS

STRAW STRAW STRAW STRAW  STRAW

LONG STORY

T
THIN
R
O
U
G
H

T
THICK
R
O
U
G
H

47

THANHEGRE

DOLOR

PROFIT   SUFFERING

EMOLUMENT   EARNINGS

ADVANTAGE   INJURY

HARM   REWARD

BENEFIT

ACHE

FRIDAY

CLOUD
CLOUD
CLOUD
CLOUD
CLOUD
CLOUD
CLOUD
HEAD
CLOUD
CLOUD

LUCIFER

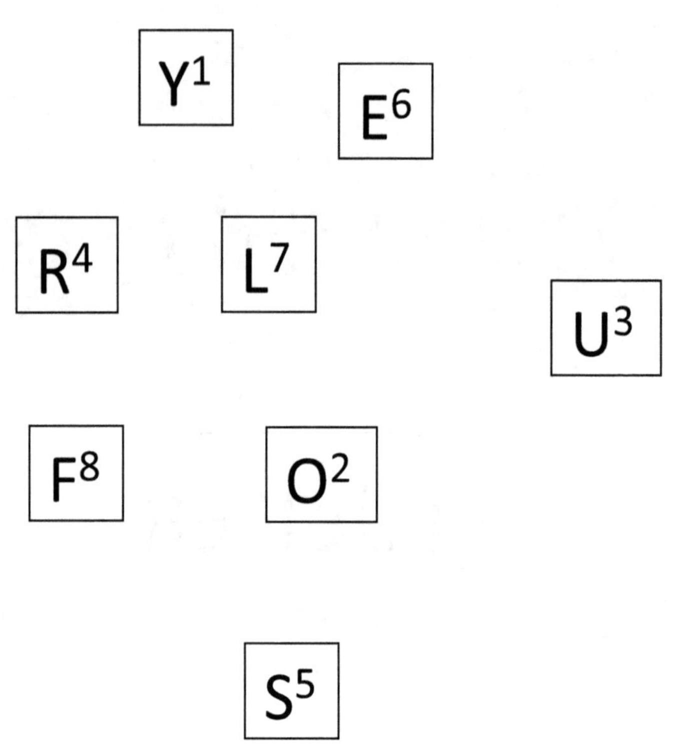

Y1
E6
R4
L7
U3
F8
O2
S5

ON

BALL

54

SPEED

=

RUBISH

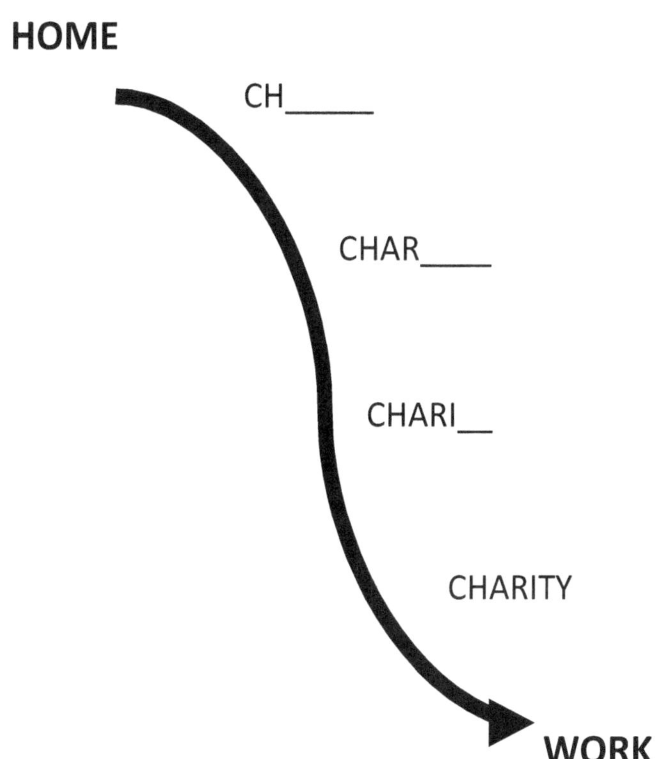

HOME
CH_____
CHAR____
CHARI__
CHARITY
WORK

INJURYINSULTINJURY

R
A
I
N

MUST

ARD

O

BLUE

T

LIE
TIE
PIE
VIE
RIE

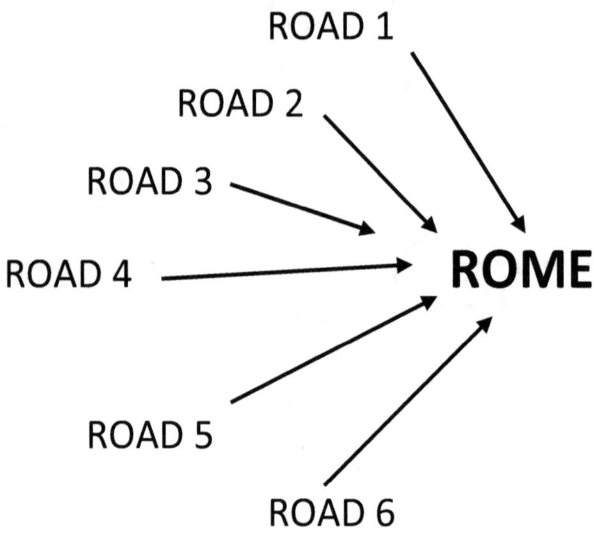

ROAD 1
ROAD 2
ROAD 3
ROAD 4
ROME
ROAD 5
ROAD 6

TRAINING

REHEARSAL

DRILL

EXERCISE

REPETITION

PERFECT

NEWS = BAD

~~NEWS~~ = GOOD

VINTAGE OLD

AGED ANTIQUE

DECREPIT ANCIENT HISTORIC

WORN OUT RAGGED

OUT OF DATE

—————————

DIAMOND

JEWELS

RUBY

ZIRCON

SILVER

RHINESTONE

20/20

HEADS

HEADS

10/20

HEAD

HAHNANDD

BABY
NOW

WANT

PANT

RANT

HANT

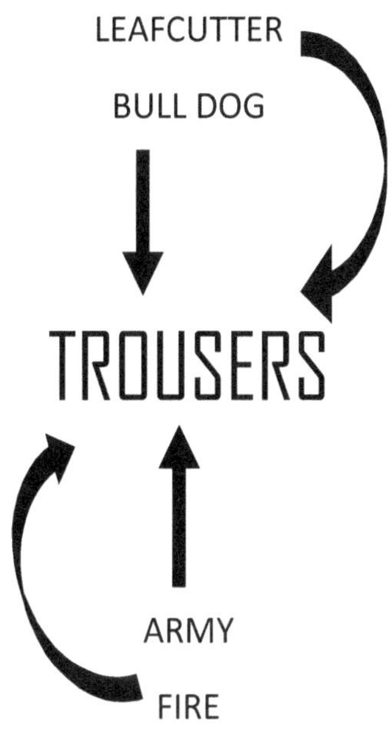

LEAFCUTTER
BULL DOG
TROUSERS
ARMY
FIRE

YOU ARE
HERE

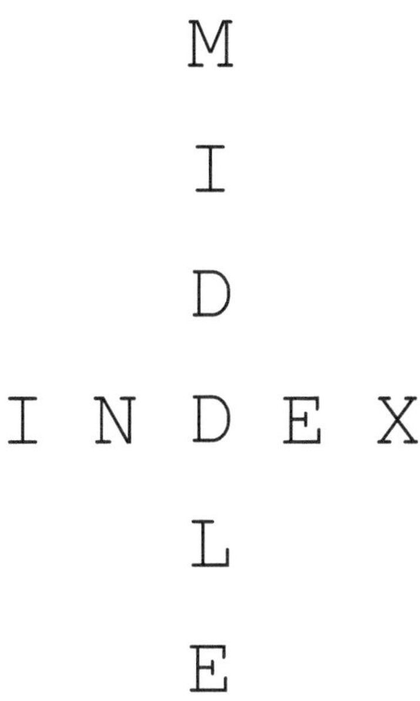
M
I
D
INDEX
D
L
E

APPEARANCES

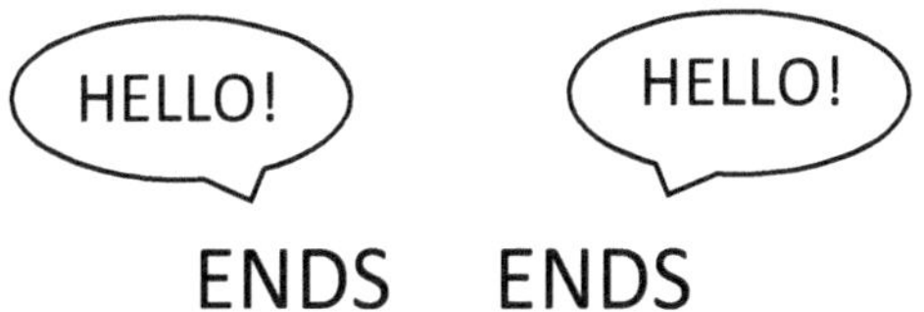

ENDS
ENDS
HELLO!
HELLO!
ENDS
ENDS

LIFE

DEATH

EEL

CARP

PIKE

SALMON

COD

MACKEREL

SEA-BREAM

SEA-BASS...

(2 X NO) + (2 X THROUGH)

BITTEN   TIMID

                TIMID

L_AST

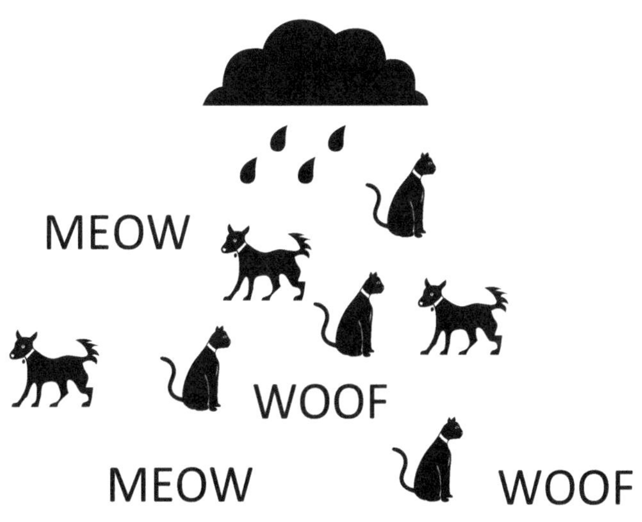

MEOW
WOOF
MEOW
WOOF

MAIGHT

MAIT

MIGHT

MITE

MIET

THAT

THAT

CAT

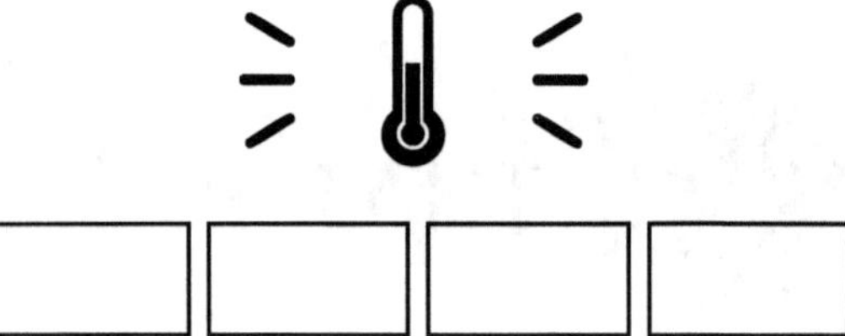

ADVOCATE

YOU

LL&RNVIEEA

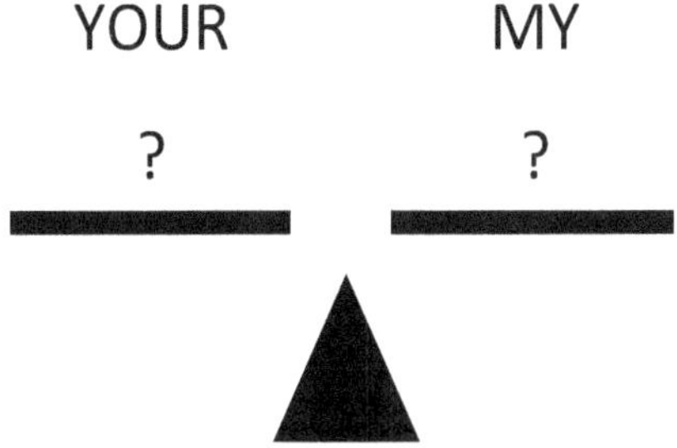

YOUR
MY
?
?

92

STROM

MOSTR

SOTRM

STORM

MTRSO

SORMT

1 NO NO 1

1   2   3   4

CHICKEN CHICKEN CHICKEN CHICKEN ....

WATER,
PLEASE !
HORSE

Page	Idiom	Meaning
cover	You can't judge a book by its cover	This person or thing may look bad, but it's good inside
3	Put something on ice	Put a project on hold
4	A storm in a teacup	A big fuss about a small problem
5	On thin ice	On probation. If you make another mistake, there will be trouble.
6	It's a piece of cake	It's easy
7	The whole nine yards	Everything, all the way.
8	The elephant in the room	The big issue, the problem people are avoiding
9	It costs an arm and a leg	It's very expensive
10	The devil is in the details	It looks good from a distance, but when you look closer, there are problems

Page	Idiom	Meaning
11	To move heaven and earth	To work very hard to do something
12	We see eye to eye	We agree
13	Spill the beans	Give away a secret
14	Look before you leap	Take only calculated risks
15	Slow and steady wins the race	Reliability is more important than speed
16	Brass Monkey Weather	Very cold weather that is extremely out of the ordinary
17	United we stand, divided we fall	If we work together we can be successful, if we fight each other we will fall
18	Turn turtle	To flip over, to turn upside down
19	To be blue	To be depressed or sad
20	Throw caution to the wind	Take a risk

Page	Idiom	Meaning
21	It's no picnic	It's difficult, it(s no fun
22	Wrap your head around something	Understand something complicated
23	To put a bug in the ear	To give someone a hint about something
24	Sacred cow	A person, thing or belief that is unreasonably above criticism or immune from questioning
25	There is a snake in the grass	There's a deceitful or treacherous person
26	To put a cat among the pigeons	To do or say something that is likely to cause alarm, controversy, or unrest among a lot of people
27	To have butterflies in the stomach	To be anxious or nervous
28	Once in a blue moon	Extremely rarely

GUESS THE HIDDEN ENGLISH IDIOMS

Page	Idiom	Meaning
29	A little bird told me	You are not going to say how you found out about something or who told it to you
30	Eager beaver	An overly enthusiastic person, someone who is overzealous and excited about doing a job
31	To be out of the wood	To be out of the wood
32	Break a leg	Good luck
33	Get out of hand	Get out of control
34	Go down in flames	Fail spectacularly
35	Better late than never	Better to arrive late than not to come at all
36	Cut somebody some slack	Don't be so critical
37	Cutting corners	Doing something poorly in order to save time or money
38	Thick as thieves	Very close friends

Page	Idiom	Meaning
39	Every cloud has a silver lining	Good things come after bad things
40	Bite the bullet	To get something over with because it is inevitable
41	A blessing in disguise	a good thing that seemed bad at first
42	There's a method to his madness	He seems crazy but actually he's clever
43	That's the last straw	My patience has run out
44	Earworm	A catchy tune or song that you can't get out of your head
45	Make a long story short	Tell something briefly
46	Through thick and thin	In good times and in bad times
47	Hang in there	Don't give up
48	No pain, no gain	You have to work for what you want

Page	Idiom	Meaning
49	Call it a day	Stop working on something
50	Have your head in the clouds	Not be concentrating
51	Speak of the devil	The person we were just talking about showed up!
52	Pull yourself together	Calm down
53	On the ball	Doing a good job
54	Haste makes waste	You'll make mistakes if you rush through something
55	Charity begins at home	A person's first responsibility is for the needs of their own family and friends
56	Add insult to injury	To make a bad situation worse
57	Break the ice	Make people feel more comfortable
58	As right as rain	Perfect

Page	Idiom	Meaning
59	Cut the mustard	Do a good job
60	Out of the blue	Randomly, unexpectedly
61	Never say die	Expression used to encourage someone to continue something or to remain hopeful
62	All the roads lead to Rome	All choices, methods, or actions eventually lead to the same result
63	Practice makes perfect	People become better at something if they do it often
64	No news is good news	One is told only the bad things about something
65	There is nothing new under the sun	There is nothing in the world that has not already happened, been seen, or been created
66	Draw the line	Stop, know the point where something goes from okay to not okay
67	All that glitters is not gold	The things that seem most valuable on the

Page	Idiom	Meaning
		surface – like gold – are often deceptive
68	Two heads are better than one	When two people work together they are more likely to solve a problem than one person doing it alone
69	Hand in hand	When two people or things are very closely connected or related
70	Not born yesterday	Used to say that someone is unlikely to believe something that is not true or to trust someone who is not trustworthy
71	There's no such word as can't	When you have self-limiting beliefs about what you can (or cannot) do, it can prevent you from going for the things that you really want to do
72	It's a small world	Used to show surprise when one meets someone one knows at

Page	Idiom	Meaning
		an unexpected place or finds out that one shares a friend, acquaintance, etc., with another person
73	To have got ants in pants	To be unable to sit still or remain calm out of nervousness or excitement
74	Under the weather	Sick
75	To cross one's fingers	To wish for luck by crossing two fingers of one hand
76	To keep up appearances	To hide something bad by pretending that nothing is wrong
77	To make ends meet	To pay for the things that you need to live when you have little money
78	As pale as death	Exceptionally pale, as due to nausea or fear
79	There are other	It's ok to miss this

Page	Idiom	Meaning
	fish in the sea	opportunity. Others will arise.
80	To know through and through	To know completely and to the greatest extent possible
81	Once bitten, twice shy	You're more cautious when you've been hurt before
82	Last but not least	Used to say that a final statement is not less important than previous statements
83	It's raining cats and dogs	It's raining hard
84	Might is right	Used to say that people who have power are able to do what they want because no one can stop them
85	You can say that again	That's true, I agree
86	To be like a cat on hot bricks	To be restless, unable to remain still

Page	Idiom	Meaning
87	Play devil's advocate	To argue the opposite, just for the sake of argument
88	Snowed under	Busy
89	Well begun is half done	Getting a good start is important
90	Live and learn	I made a mistake
91	Your guess is as good as mine	I have no idea
92	A perfect storm	the worst possible situation
93	It takes one to know one	Someone must have a bad quality themselves if they can recognize it in other people
94	Don't count your chickens before they hatch	Don't count on something good happening until it's happened.
95	You can lead a horse to water, but you can't make him drink	You can't force someone to make the right decision

Page	Idiom	Meaning
96	Time flies when you're having fun	You don't notice how long something lasts when it's fun

9 782957 585410